WITHDRAWN

Presented to
the
SAINT PAUL
PUBLIC
LIBRARY

by

The Thomas Y. Crowell
Company

Archimedes
Takes a Bath

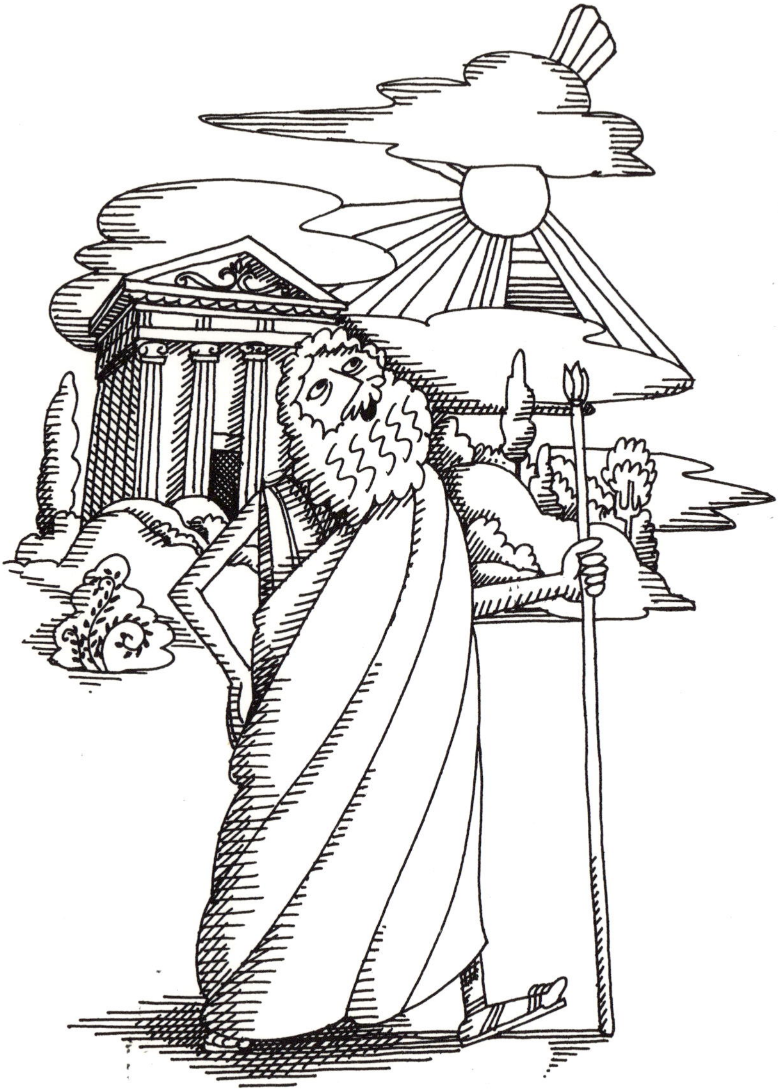

Archimedes Takes a Bath

BY JOAN M. LEXAU

Illustrated by Salvatore Murdocca

Thomas Y. Crowell Company   New York

Copyright © 1969 by Joan M. Lexau
Illustrations Copyright © 1969
by Salvatore Murdocca

All rights reserved. Except for use in a review, the reproduction or utilization of this work in any form or by any electronic, mechanical, or other means, now known or hereafter invented, including xerography, photocopying, and recording, and in any information storage and retrieval system is forbidden without the written permission of the publisher.

Manufactured in the United States of America
L.C. Card 69-11084

1 2 3 4 5 6 7 8 9 10

To John M. Hinds

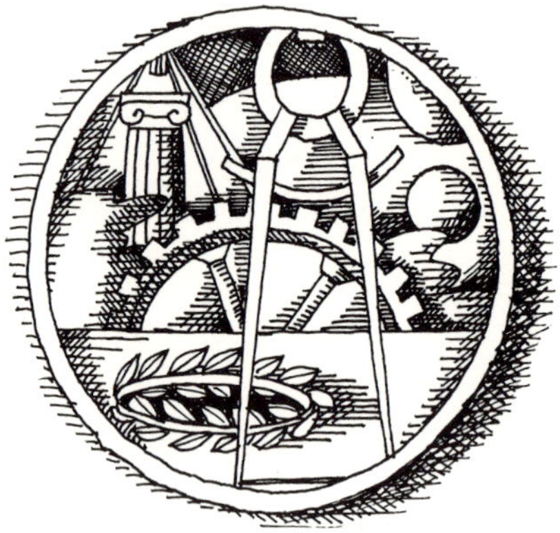

"Stop! What are you doing to my cousin?" said the king of Syracuse. "Why are you pulling and pushing him that way?"

"Sire, it is the only way we can get him to the Baths," said the slaves.

"Archimedes, when did you last take a bath?" asked King Hiero.

"Why, it must have been this morning, was it not?" Archimedes asked the slaves.

"This morning!" one of them said. "You have not had a bath for weeks. It is all we can do to get you to eat now and then."

The king said, "You must have a bath every day. I know, I know—for you there is no such thing as time. You are always busy thinking, and this is a good thing. But you must eat and you must take a bath. Go and do it now."

"Yes, sire," said Archimedes. He went away with the slaves.

The king shook his head and walked up and down, thinking. Then he said, "Send me the boy slave, Xanthius."

Xanthius came and stood before him.

The king said, "Xanthius, I hear good things of you. Now I have a job for you to do. Do you know my cousin Archimedes?"

Xanthius said, "The one who goes about in a dream?"

"Yes, that is Archimedes," said the king.

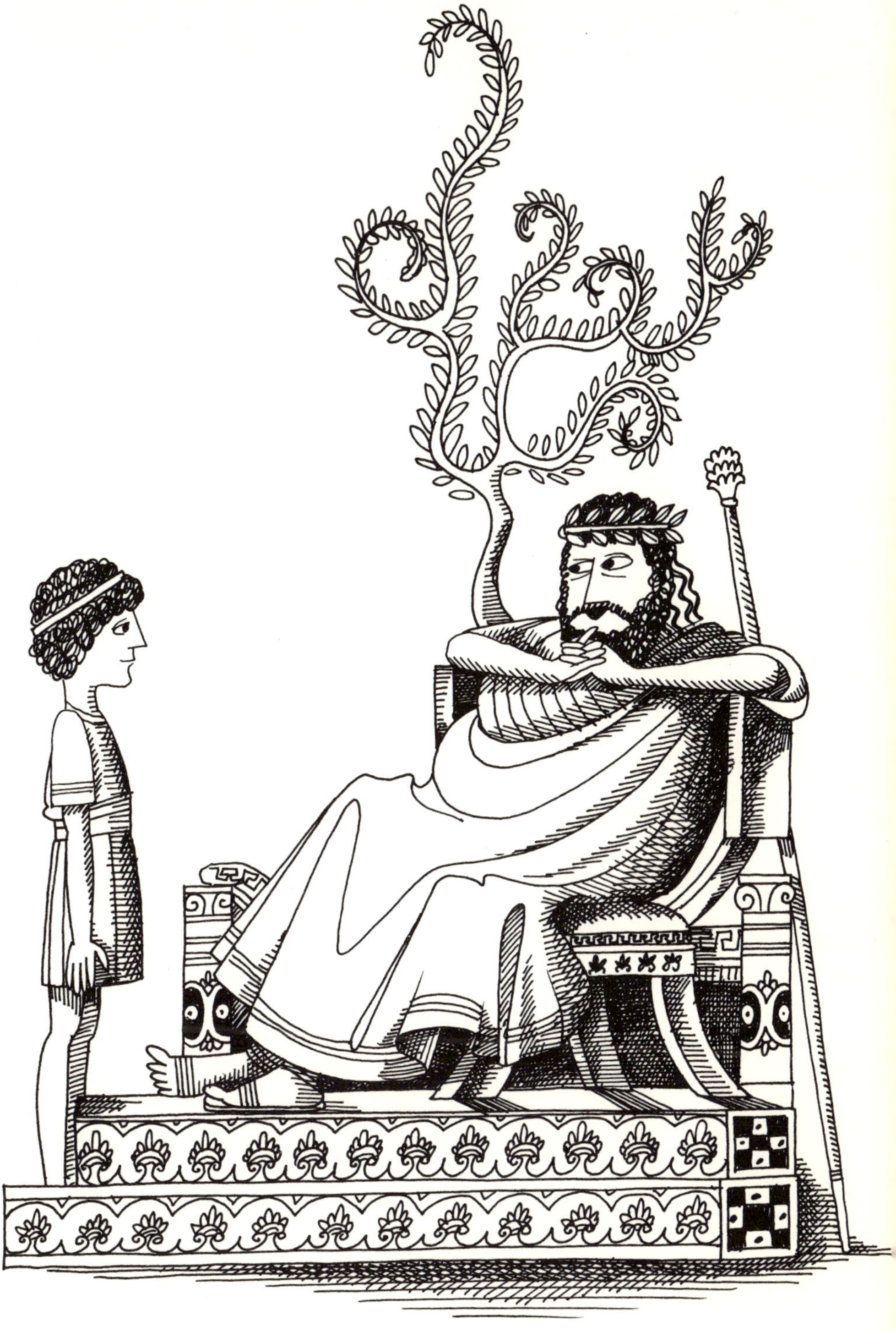

"He is not a man like other men. He dreams dreams that none have ever dreamed before. His father found out how big the sun and moon are, but Archimedes can tell you how far the sun and the moon and the planets are from each other and much more as well."

"I am told that he is the one who found me," said Xanthius.

"Yes," said the king. "There you were, a few days old, in a pot by the market. Your parents had put you there as many do, not wanting you because they already had one or two children, but hoping someone would want you. Archimedes was walking along—not looking where he was going, the way he does—and he fell over you. He brought you to me. He said he could not leave you there after falling over you. So I let my slaves bring you up. Now I want you to help the man who saved your life."

"But how can I do that, sire?" asked Xanthius.

The king said, "Archimedes is always busy thinking, too busy to take care of himself. He forgets to eat. He does not like to take time to have a bath. In some ways he is like a child, so it may be that a child can help him."

"I will try, sire," said Xanthius. If all he had to do was tell a man when it was time to eat or take a bath, the job would be easy.

But he soon found it was not so easy.

Archimedes was sitting on the floor. There was sand all over the floor.

"Stop!" Archimedes yelled.

Xanthius stopped. What had he done?

"Get off the moon," Archimedes said.

"Yes, sire," Xanthius said. What next! He stepped to one side.

"Get off that planet!" Archimedes yelled.

Xanthius looked down. There were circles all over the floor. Archimedes was making more

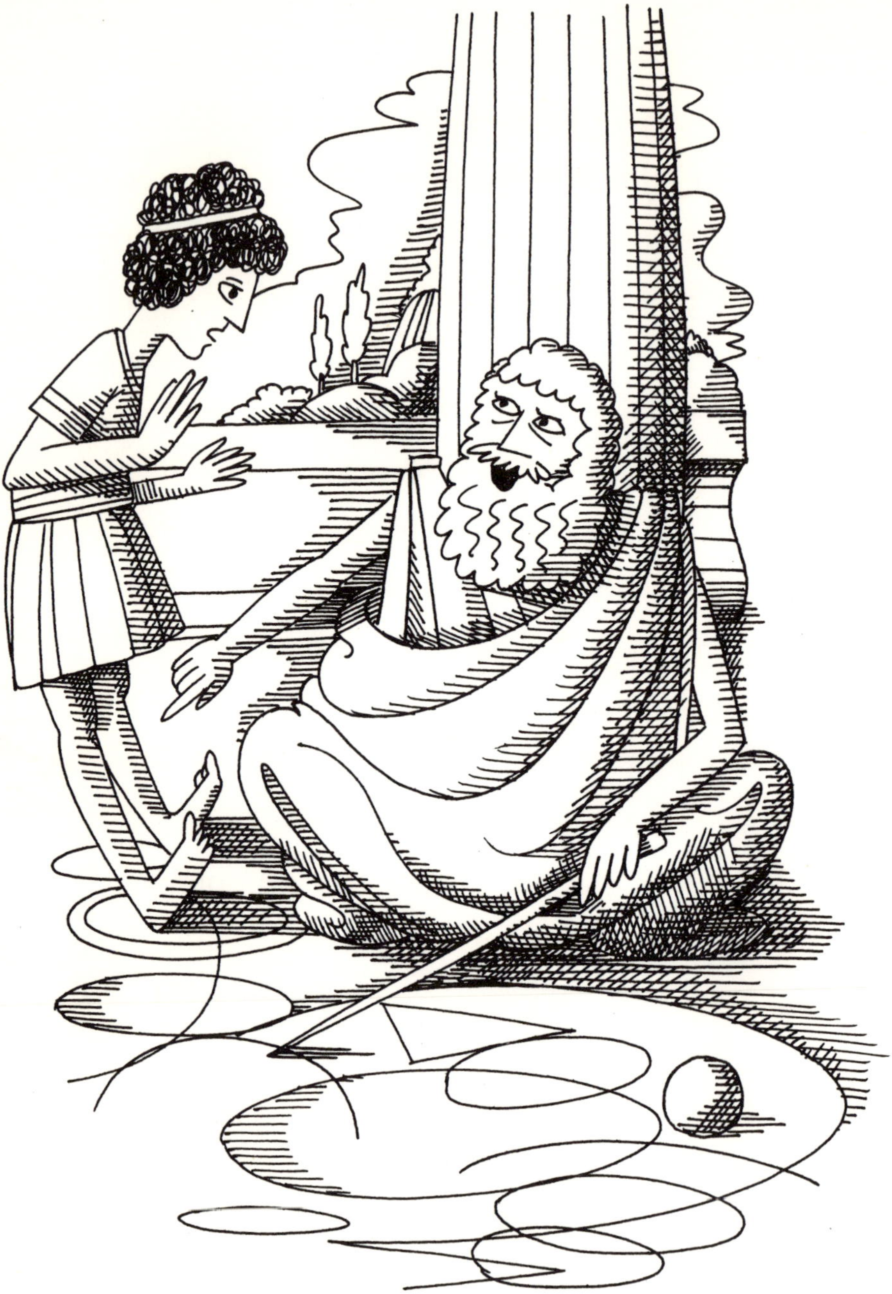

of them. In the corners of the room there were squares and triangles and many numbers.

"What do you want, boy?" Archimedes asked.

"I am come to work for you," Xanthius told him. "My name is Xanthius."

"I do not need you," Archimedes said.

"Long ago you saved my life," Xanthius said. "When I was a baby you fell over me and brought me to the king."

"I remember the baby," Archimedes said. "It is an awful thing to throw out a baby. Rich and poor, they all do it, so they can give more to the one or two children they keep. Yes, such a noise that baby made. But that was a few weeks ago. It could not have been you."

"But it was," said Xanthius. "Anyway, the king sent me."

"Hmm," said Archimedes. He was looking at the floor again. He said no more.

Xanthius looked around. At the edge of the floor there was a path. He walked along the path and sat down, not too near Archimedes. Just sat and watched.

By and by he was hungry. Maybe Archimedes was hungry too. He asked him.

"Mmm?" said Archimedes, not looking up.

"Are you hungry, sire? Do you want some food?" Xanthius said again.

"Not now. Go away. I am busy," Archimedes said.

Did a man like this know even when he was hungry? Maybe he would have to do more than just tell Archimedes when it was time to eat. Maybe he would have to make him eat somehow. Maybe this was not such an easy job after all.

Xanthius went to eat. He brought back a bowl of food for Archimedes.

"Are you hungry now?" Xanthius asked.

Archimedes just sat there, writing numbers in the sand.

Xanthius went up to Archimedes very quietly and put the bowl down. "When he is hungry, he will eat," Xanthius said to himself.

Archimedes drew a line from one circle to another. He drew a line from that circle to the bowl. He drew a line from the bowl to another circle. He shook his head.

"There is something wrong," said Archimedes.

Xanthius put his hand over his mouth to keep from laughing.

Archimedes picked up the bowl. "You are not a planet," he said. He began to eat, looking at the circles.

When Archimedes was done eating, Xanthius said, "How was the food, sire?"

"What food?" Archimedes said. "And who are you? What are you doing here?"

"But, sire, the king sent me," Xanthius began.

"Go away. Go and play," Archimedes said.

Xanthius went out. He should not have said anything. His job was to see that Archimedes ate and took a bath. If Archimedes wanted to talk, he would talk.

But Xanthius was happy. He had found a way to make Archimedes eat. It did not matter if Archimedes knew he had eaten. Just so long as he ate. Now, if he could think of a way to make Archimedes take a bath without knowing it—

Xanthius watched some boys playing with dice. Then he went over to some other boys who were kneeling around a circle. One boy tossed a stone near the center of the circle. The next boy knocked the stone away with his stone.

"Good throw," Xanthius said.

"Xanthius," someone called. "I have some clay. Do you want to make some soldiers?"

Xanthius went with his friend Droman. As they made the soldiers, they put them out in the sun to get hard. Xanthius told Droman that the king had given him a job working for Archimedes. He did not say what the job was. He did not want to say that a man like Archimedes could not look after himself.

"I had better get back," Xanthius said at last. "Archimedes may need me."

Droman began to laugh. "Need you! Archimedes knows more than you will ever know

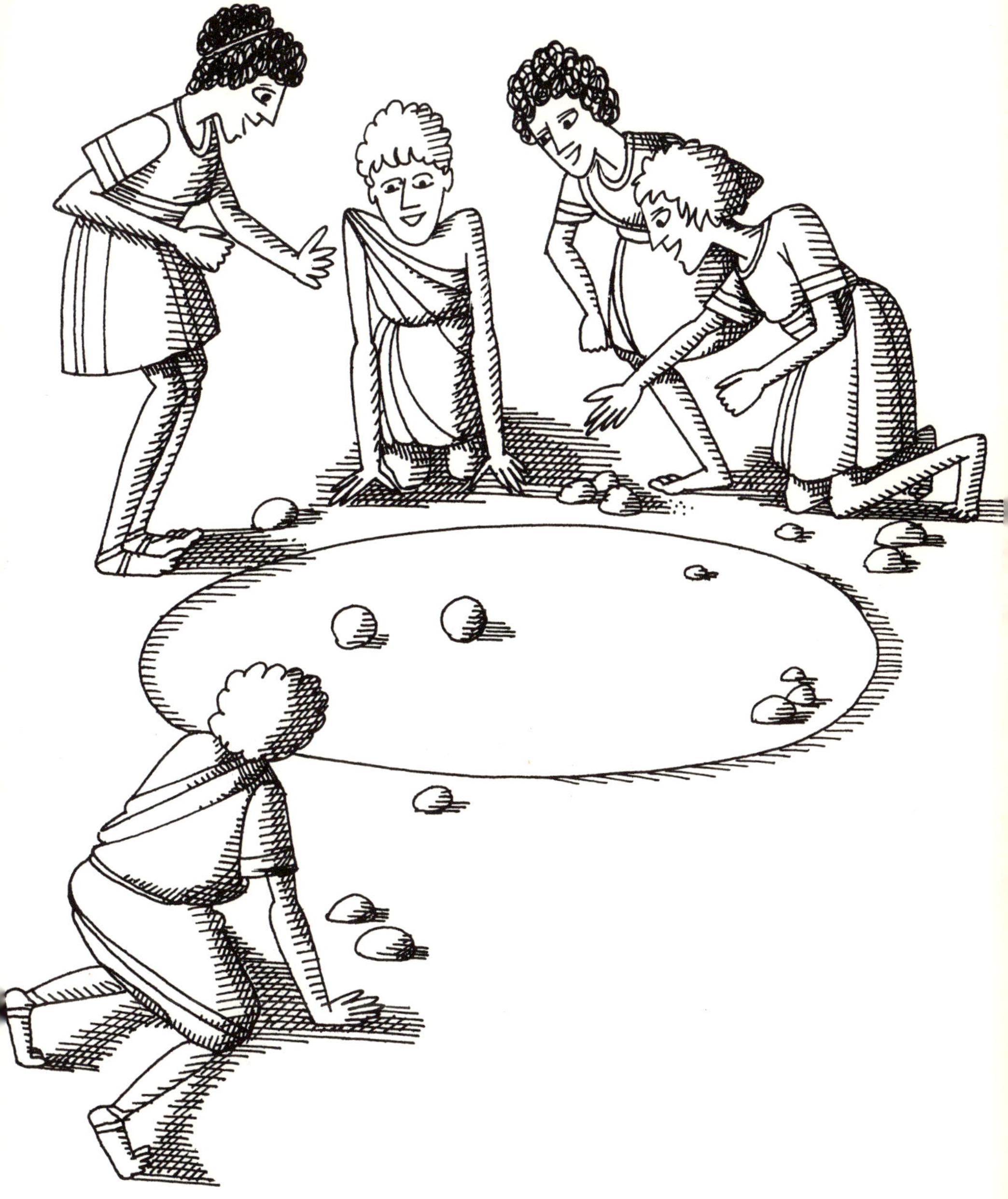

there is to know. How silly you are, Xanthius. He may let you do this and that for him but not anything big. He does not need you."

Xanthius went away, not saying anything. He was thinking, "I would rather watch Archimedes than be with you at all, Droman."

Maybe someday he could do something big for Archimedes. Someday—He laughed. Now he was dreaming dreams. Like Archimedes.

Archimedes was sitting with his eyes closed. Xanthius did not know if he was asleep. He went in very quietly and sat in a corner.

"You may have that corner to draw in," said Archimedes. "What is your name?"

"Xanthius, sire."

"Come here. I will show you something," Archimedes said.

Xanthius walked along the path and sat down next to Archimedes. What he saw was a machine made up of many metal balls.

"The one in the center is the earth, of course," said Archimedes. "The others are the sun and the moon and the five planets. Here are Saturn and Mars and Jupiter and Venus, and that one is Mercury. Turn this lever, boy. Did you tell me your name?"

"Xanthius, sire," he said again. He turned the lever. The metal balls began to move. The sun and the moon and the planets went around, each in its own path at its own speed.

"There is a man who says that the earth and the planets go around the sun, that the sun is in the center," Archimedes said. "Does that seem right to you?"

Archimedes was asking him! Was he joking? He did not seem to be. So Xanthius had better think about this and not say anything silly.

"Well," Xanthius said at last, "we can see the sun come up and go across the sky and go down, so the earth must be in the center. We can see that the sun goes around us."

"That is what I keep telling myself," said Archimedes. "But if the earth was going around the sun, and if, at the same time, the earth was turning, would it not look the way it does? Our eyes can fool us."

"Mmm," said Xanthius. He did not know what else to say. He and Archimedes looked at the metal balls going around.

"Did you make this?" Xanthius asked. "It is a wonderful thing."

Archimedes said, "The king is always telling me to make things that are of some use, things the people can see. So I do it. Sometime I will show you other things I am making. But I do not want to make things, I want to think about ideas. Ideas have beauty. Even if we cannot see the beauty, we can feel it. I do not care about things but about the ideas behind the things. Do you see?"

"Well—" said Xanthius.

Archimedes pointed to the metal ball that was the earth. "If you found a ball like this, what would you think? That you could roll it and play with it or make some use of it. But I would think, if I did not know already:

How can I measure that ball? How can I find out how wide it is at its widest part? How can I figure out how much metal is in it? How can I—"

His eyes were looking at nothing. He was thinking again. Xanthius did not tell him he would like to play with the ball and measure it too. He went to his own corner.

How, Xanthius asked himself, how do you get a man who is thinking about things like that to think about taking a bath?

The next day he was again able to get Archimedes to eat by putting food near him and saying nothing. But he could not bring the Baths to Archimedes. He would have to bring Archimedes to the Baths. How?

Xanthius went for a walk to think about it.

Someone called his name. He turned.

"Xanthius, what are you doing out? Archimedes needs you. He wants you to bring him the moon." It was Droman.

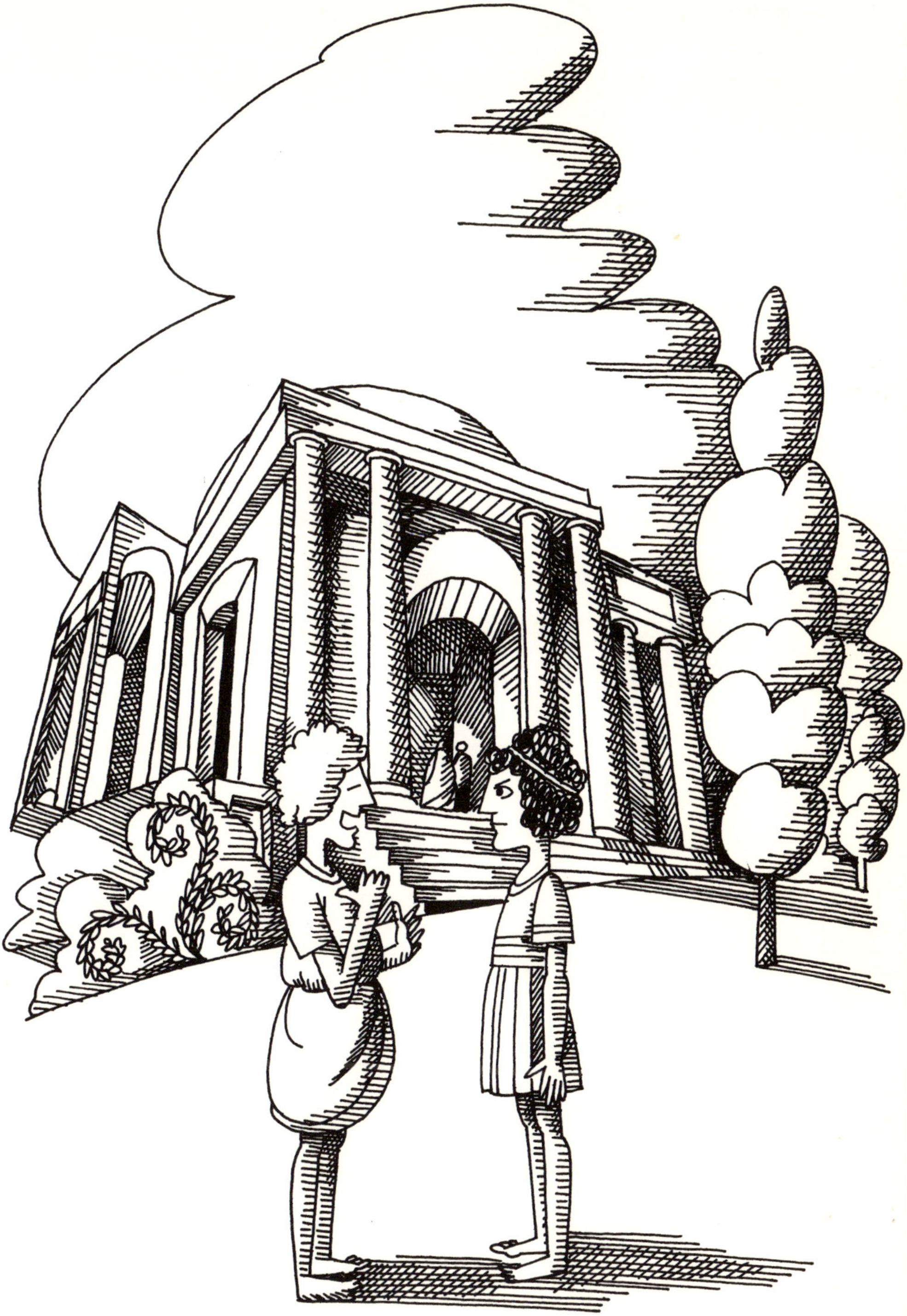

Xanthius turned his back and went on walking.

"I am sorry, Xanthius," Droman said. "I did not mean it. Come and play."

Xanthius stopped. He was by the Baths.

That was it! All he had to do was get Archimedes to take a walk by the Baths. If Xanthius just walked in, maybe Archimedes would follow. And, Archimedes being Archimedes, maybe he would then take a bath without thinking about it.

"What is it, Xanthius? You look funny," Droman said.

"Hmm?" said Xanthius.

He ran back. Archimedes was writing numbers in the sand, numbers longer than any Xanthius had ever seen.

"He is busy. I will wait," Xanthius told himself. He went to his corner and played with his clay soldiers.

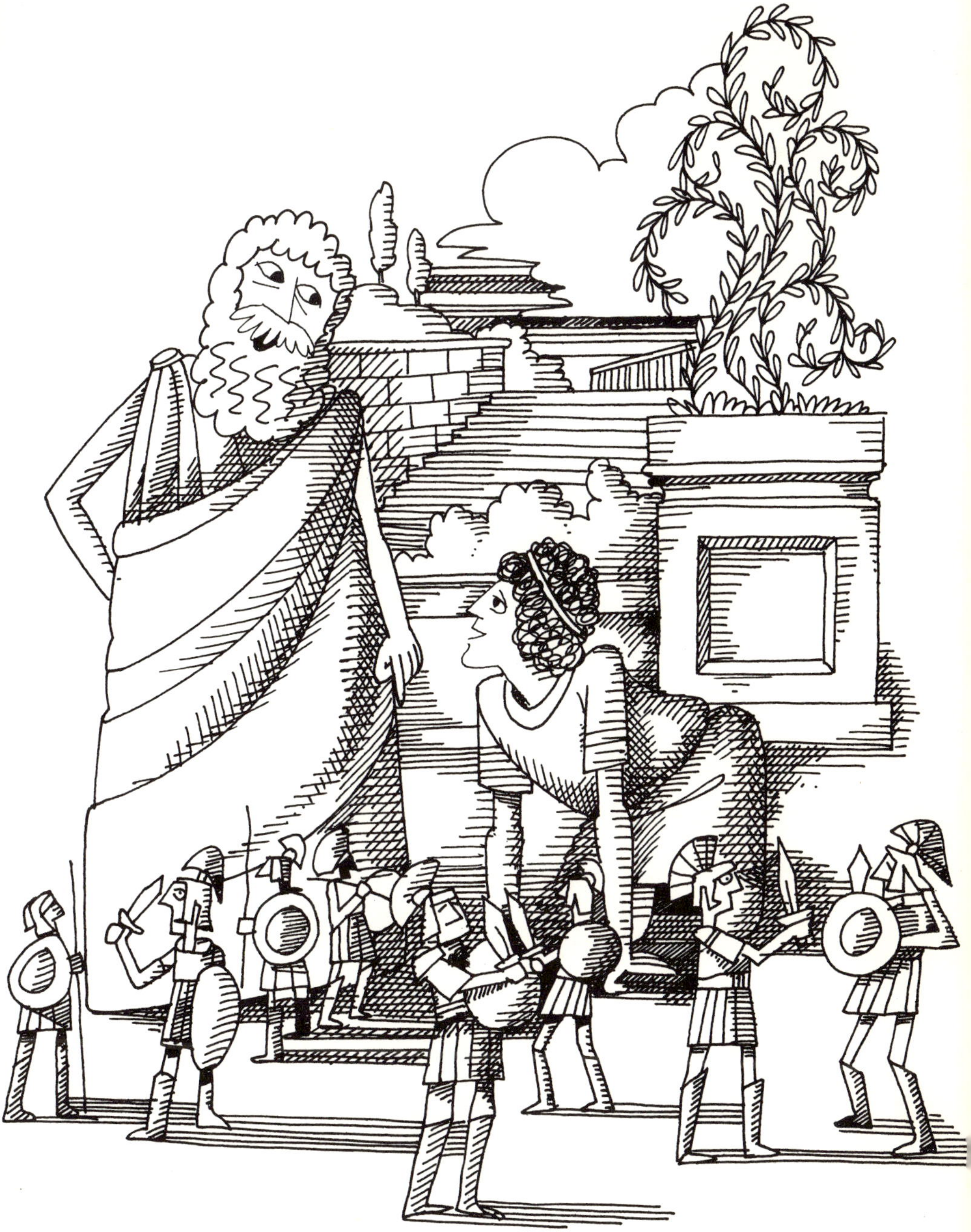

A great battle was going on when he heard Archimedes say, "Which one is the general?"

Xanthius looked up. Archimedes was watching him.

"I am the general, sire."

"Good," said Archimedes. "That is what the king was before he was made king."

"He is a good king," Xanthius said. "I hear that he has never hurt anyone or killed anyone or made anyone go away from Syracuse. That is something for a king."

"I remember when he was a general," Archimedes said quietly as if to himself. "I remember when he had some soldiers he did not trust. He did not kill them. He sent them into a battle he knew they could not win. He did not kill them, but they all died."

Xanthius said nothing. He did not know if Archimedes was talking to him.

Now was the time to ask Archimedes if he

wanted to take a walk. What was that noise? He looked out the door.

Rain was coming down hard.

Getting Archimedes out in a good rain might be better than nothing. On the other hand, he might catch cold.

"Would you like to have a real battle?" Archimedes asked. "Come here and see this war machine. Bring your soldiers."

Archimedes handed some clay ships to Xanthius. He said out loud but to himself, "I know his name. I have been calling him by it all these weeks. How could I forget it?"

He did not give Xanthius time to tell him his name or that he had known him for days, not weeks. He went on, "Um, you are the enemy. You come by sea in your ships. Give me half your soldiers. I did not make any."

Xanthius began pushing the ships slowly to Archimedes.

Archimedes brought out a machine Xanthius had not seen before. He pointed to his knee.

"This is the edge of the cliff," he said.

He set the machine down on the edge of the cliff and turned a lever. An iron claw on a chain came down. The claw took hold of the front of a ship and pulled it half out of the water. When the claw let go, the ship turned over.

"Good-by, ship. Good-by, soldiers," said Xanthius. "If only a real machine like that could be made, you would not have to worry about an enemy coming by sea."

"A real machine will be made, Um. I made this little one to show the king how it could be done," Archimedes said. "He asked me to make some machines that could be used in a battle."

"But it could not lift a real ship, could it? A ship is very heavy," Xanthius said.

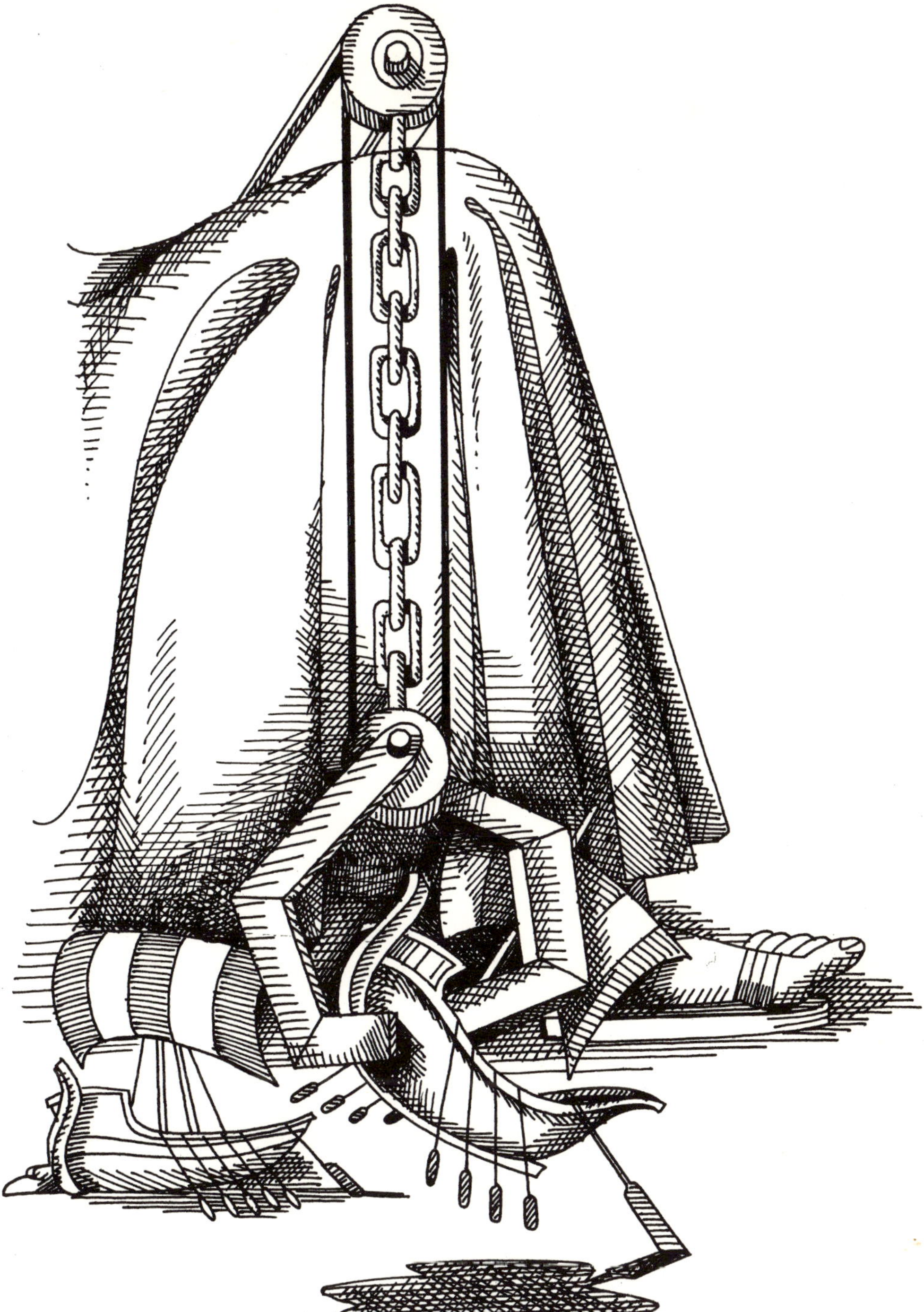

"That is what the king said. I told him that if he could find me a place to stand, I could move the earth. With levers and pulleys you can lift anything."

Archimedes sighed. "The king is always after me to make things or do things. He says I can think better than anyone he ever heard of. So why can he not leave me free to think? Why can he not be happy with the big new buildings he is having built?"

"Do you have to make things for him? What would he do if you said no?" Xanthius asked.

"Nothing, but he would be sad, and he is my king, my cousin, and my friend," said Archimedes. "Did I tell you about the mirrors?"

"Mirrors?" Xanthius asked.

"Another thing I am making for the king. There will be many mirrors set in just the right way. At noon, when the sun is nearest, they will turn the sun's rays and point them at enemy ships and set them on fire."

Xanthius did not see how that could work, but if Archimedes said he could do it, he could.

They went back to their battle. Archimedes showed Xanthius how to work the iron claw. Xanthius upset the ships and Archimedes was the enemy.

"What are you doing?"

Xanthius jumped to his feet. It was King Hiero.

The king walked with care upon the path at the edge of the floor. "I trust Syracuse is winning," he said. "Archimedes, I have a problem." He had with him a golden crown.

"I had this made so I could put it in the temple to give thanks to the gods for being chosen king. But word has come to me that the maker of the crown may have kept some of the gold I gave him to use for the crown. He may have put some silver in its place."

"Can you tell me how much gold you gave him, sire? I will weigh the crown," Archimedes said.

"Cousin, even I thought of that," King Hiero said. "It weighs what it should weigh."

"Ah, you think he left out some gold and

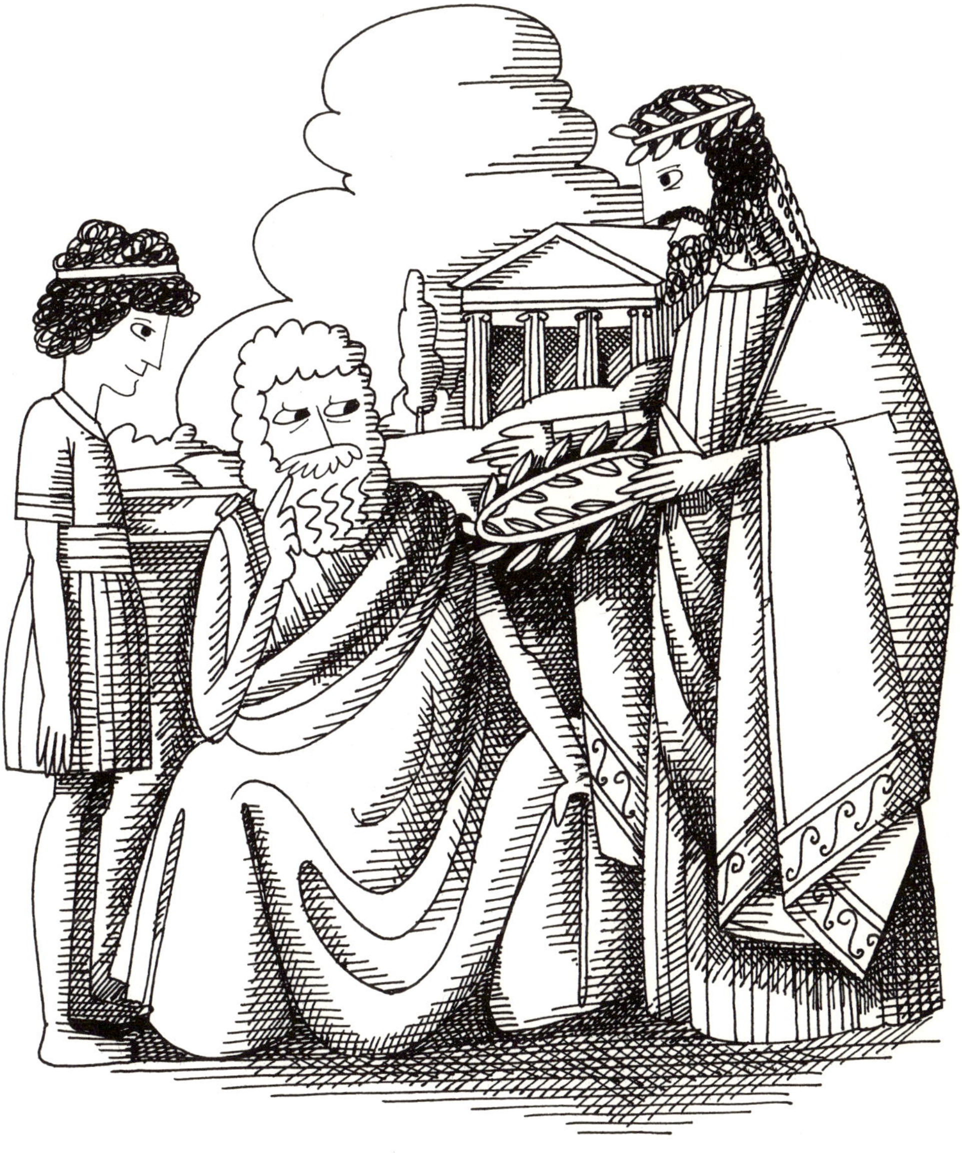

put in a greater amount of silver?" Archimedes asked.

"It may be," the king said. "I do not know how to find out. That is the problem."

"I see," Archimedes said.

Xanthius did not see. He tried to figure it out. The king and Archimedes went on talking. Just as Xanthius gave up, he heard the king say, "How is this boy doing? Is he in your way?"

"Hmm?" said Archimedes. He was looking at the crown and turning it over.

"Xanthius, is Archimedes eating?" the king asked.

"Yes, sire."

"Did he have a bath today?" the king asked.

Xanthius hung his head.

"If he eats, that is something," the king said. "Keep trying."

"Yes, sire," Xanthius said.

Archimedes did not see the king go out. He was turning the crown around and around and talking to himself.

"Gold weighs more than silver," he said. "So to keep the crown the same weight, the crown maker would have had to add a larger amount of silver than the gold he took out. So I need to know how much metal is in the crown."

This was no time to ask Archimedes if he wanted to take a walk. It was too late in the day anyway.

The next day began badly. Archimedes walked and he talked and he sat and he talked and he walked and he talked, all the time holding on to the king's crown. He even left the path and walked in the center of the floor. He messed up planets and numbers all over the floor.

31

Xanthius could not stand to see him this way. Without thinking, he cried out, "Sire, can I do something?" Then he turned red. What could he do? He was still trying to figure out just what the problem was.

Archimedes smiled. "You can listen while I talk, Um. Then people cannot say I am talking to myself. I will tell you what the problem is, just as if you did not know. It will help me to see it better. Let us go for a walk."

"A walk, yes! Yes, a walk," Xanthius said. Here was his chance. He would take Archimedes to the Baths. There Archimedes could take a bath and talk about the problem of the crown.

Archimedes turned another way.

"How about this way, sire?" Xanthius said.

"I want to walk to the cliff and look at the sea. It helps me think sometimes," Archimedes said.

To himself Xanthius said, "Well, I tried."

"What was that?" asked Archimedes.

Xanthius sighed. Now *he* was thinking out loud.

"Nothing," he said.

Archimedes walked very fast. Xanthius almost had to run to keep up. At last they sat down under a tree. Archimedes put the crown on the ground.

"Look at this crown," he said. "How much metal is in it?"

"I do not know, sire," Xanthius said. How could he know?

"Ah, that is the problem," Archimedes said. "I know how much gold should be in it. But how can I measure a thing that goes this way and that way? Um, bring me some stones."

"Stones?" Xanthius said.

"Little stones," Archimedes said.

Xanthius did as he was told but he wished

Archimedes would talk some more about the problem of the crown.

He went back with the stones and gave them to Archimedes. Archimedes gave most of them back to Xanthius.

"You are the crown maker," he said. "I am giving you this gold to make the crown."

"Oh," Xanthius said.

"But you want to steal some gold. Take some of the gold away," Archimedes said.

Xanthius took a few stones away.

"Now," Archimedes said, "you know the king will weigh the crown to see if you have taken some gold. You want it to weigh what the gold weighed. So you will have to add some metal."

"Yes, sire," said Xanthius.

"You will add some silver. The king will not be able to tell by looking at the crown. But silver is not as heavy as gold. So you will have to add more silver than the gold you took out."

"Of course," Xanthius said. Now he saw. Archimedes gave him some stones to add to the pile, more stones than Xanthius had just taken out.

Archimedes said, "If the crown were made of stones, I could count them. Or I could measure it if it were one of those dice you boys play with. I could measure how wide the dice was and how high and how deep. But this crown—" He turned the crown around and around. Xanthius said nothing.

Archimedes went on, "I could melt it and measure it in pints or make it into a brick and measure the bricks. The king would not care for that. But I could get the king to give me a block of gold the same size as the one he gave the crown maker. And if I could melt the crown and make a block of it, I could put the two blocks side by side and see which one was larger. If the block from the crown was larger, I would know that silver had been added to it."

He stopped talking and looked at the sea. Xanthius was very quiet. It was all he could do to help.

He was almost asleep when Archimedes got up and walked away. Xanthius started after him.

"Oops," he said. Archimedes had left the crown. Xanthius went back for it. Dare he carry it himself? Archimedes was far ahead.

Xanthius picked up the crown and ran after Archimedes. The crown was heavy.

"This is a heavy thing to put on a head," Xanthius said. He looked around. No one was looking. Did he dare?

Xanthius slowed down and put the crown on as he walked. The crown was too big and came over his eyes. He took another step and fell.

"Ouch!" he cried.

Someone took the crown off his head. It was Archimedes and he was laughing.

"You need a smaller crown or a bigger head," he said.

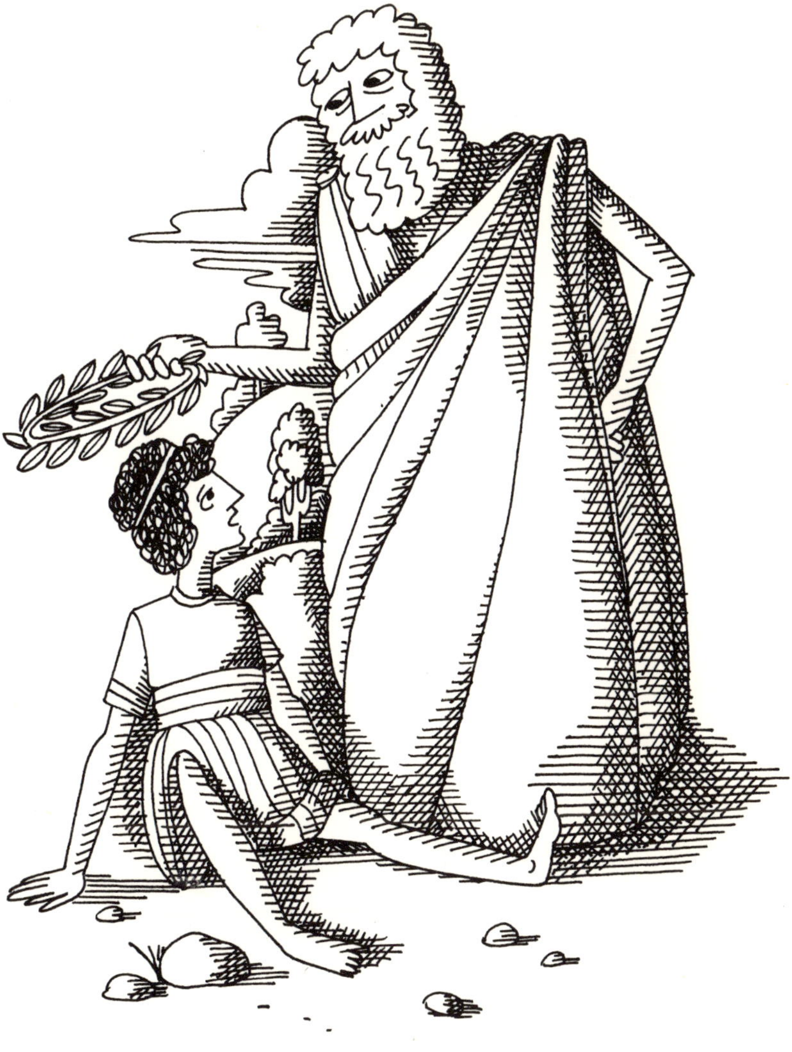

That was the last word Archimedes said to Xanthius for days.

He walked and he talked to himself—but not a word to Xanthius. He bumped into buildings and said "I am so sorry." Xanthius walked after him and watched him but he did not try to talk to him.

When the king came to see Archimedes and asked how he was doing, Archimedes said, "Go away. I am busy."

Xanthius ran after the king. "Sire, he does not know what he is saying. He does not know who you are."

"I know that," said King Hiero. "I have never seen him this bad before. But there is nothing I can do. I cannot tell him to stop thinking about the crown. I do not think he could make himself stop."

That was the day Archimedes stopped eating the food Xanthius put in front of him. He pushed the bowl away. Many hours later the food was still there.

Xanthius began to cry. He could not help it. What on earth could he do to make Archimedes eat? He was ready to give up. Maybe he should tell the king he could not do the job.

Someone was shaking him. "What is it? Are you ill?" Archimedes asked.

"No, but you will be if you do not eat," Xanthius said.

"I am not hungry. Later I will eat. I will be all right," said Archimedes.

Later, for Archimedes, could mean days.

Xanthius said, "Then I will not eat until you do, sire, and I am very hungry."

"Bring me some food and I will eat it," Archimedes said.

Xanthius went to get more food. Archimedes ate it at once.

41

"Now, is that all that upset you?" he asked.

"Well—there is one more thing," Xanthius said.

"What is that?" Archimedes asked.

"Well, sire, it—it has been a long time since you had a bath."

"Not a long time, Um. A day or two maybe," Archimedes said.

Xanthius had an idea. "You could take a bath and think about how many drops of water are in the tub." It would do him good to stop thinking about the crown.

"How many drops of water in a tub! When I have been working on the problem of how many grains of sand would fill up the universe!" Archimedes said, smiling.

"Oh," said Xanthius. "I did not know there were any numbers that big."

"There were not," Archimedes said. "I have had to give them names as I went along. And

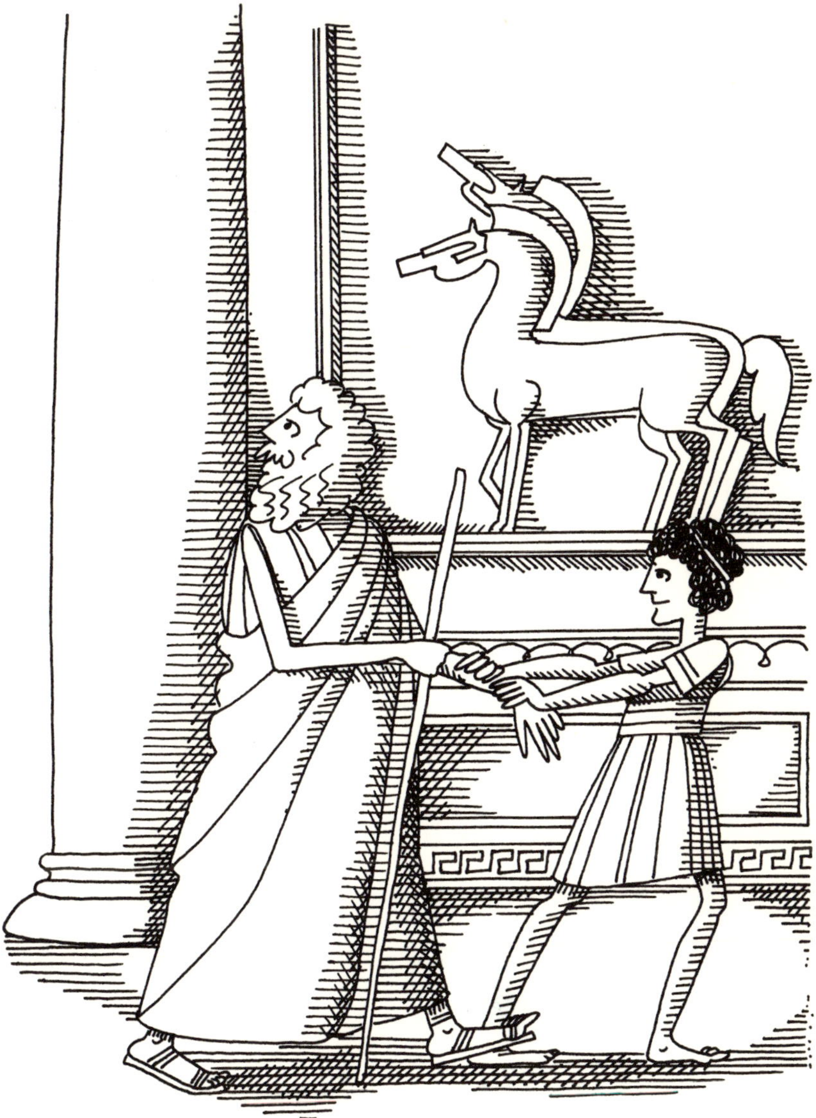

just now I am very busy working out this problem of the crown. The answer could come to me any time now, just like that. The more I think about it, the sooner it will come."

"But, sire, you can do both," Xanthius said.

"Both?" said Archimedes.

"Take a bath and think, sire. You can do both at the same time. Why not?" asked Xanthius.

"You know, I think you may be right," Archimedes said. He was out the door before Xanthius was on his feet. Xanthius ran after him.

In the Baths, Archimedes took off his clothes and threw them to Xanthius.

The tub was full. As Archimedes got in, water ran over the top. Archimedes sat down. More water ran out.

"Did you see that? Um, did you see that?" Archimedes cried.

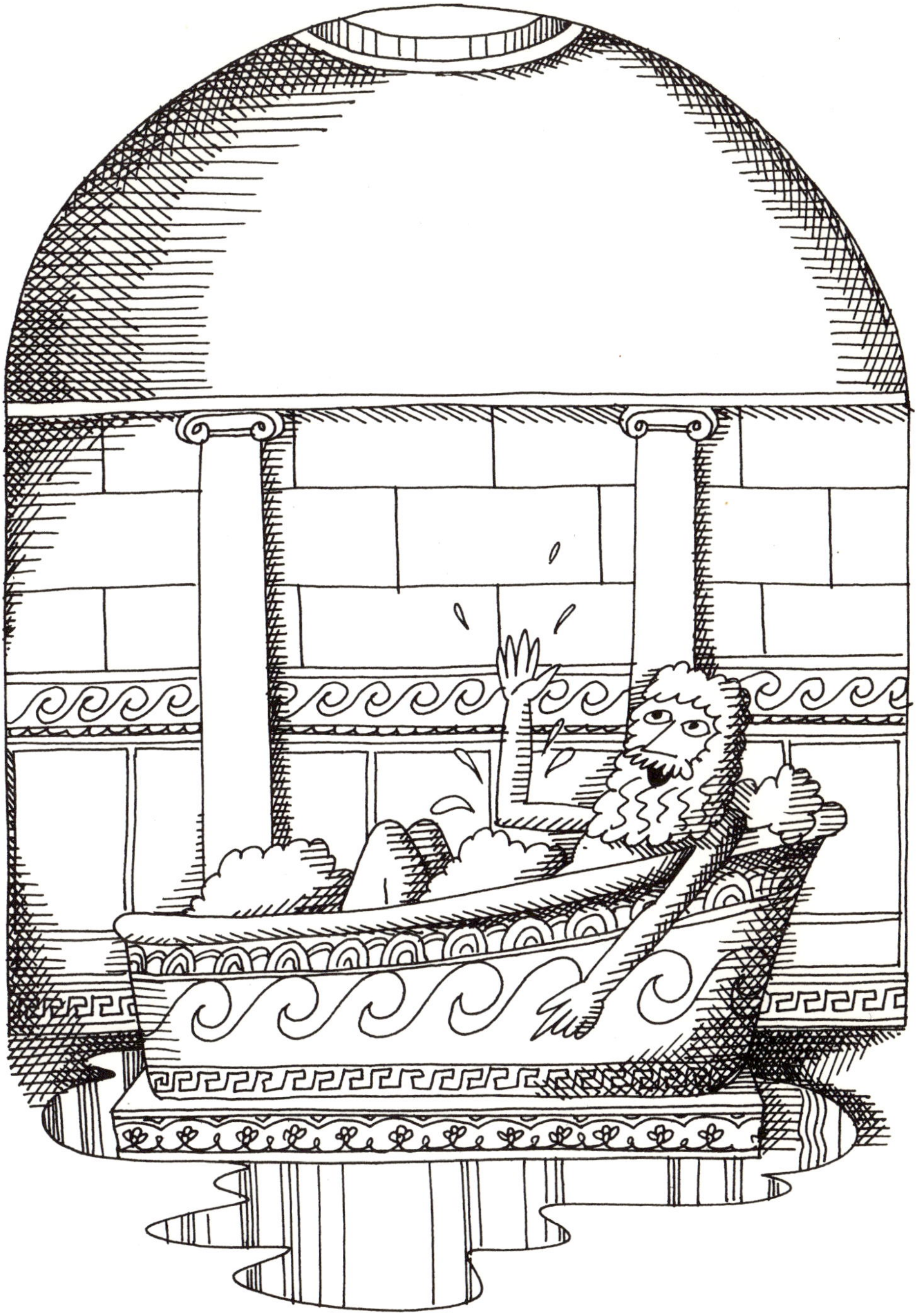

"See what, sire? What is it?" Xanthius asked.

"The water! The water! As much water ran out as there is me in the tub!"

Archimedes jumped out of the tub and ran out of the Baths yelling, "Eureka! Eureka!" which means "I have it! I have it!"

Xanthius ran after him, waving his clothes in the air and screaming, "Sire, THERE IS SOMETHING YOU DO NOT HAVE!"

All the time he was thinking to himself,

"This problem of the crown has made him go mad."

He heard someone say, "Xanthius, he needs you." It was Droman, of course. He was laughing so hard he had fallen on the ground.

Xanthius wished he had time to stop and give Droman a kick but he ran on.

Xanthius did not catch up to Archimedes until they were back in his room.

"Well, he is dry by now," Xanthius said. He threw the clothes over Archimedes' head.

"Go to the king and tell him I need some gold, the same weight as the crown. And a large bowl," Archimedes said.

Xanthius ran. He did not know if the king would give him these things just for the asking. Or if the king would even see him.

The king saw him right away. Xanthius told him what Archimedes needed.

"Bring them," the king said to the slaves, and they were brought to him.

"Does he have the answer?" the king asked Xanthius.

"He has the answer or he is mad," Xanthius said.

"I am told he took a bath. A very quick bath," the king said.

With a red face, Xanthius said, "Yes, sire."

The king laughed. "Let us see what he is going to do now." He helped to carry the things.

When they got to Archimedes' room he was not there. Soon he came in with a large jug of water.

Without saying anything, he filled the bowl to the top with water from the jug.

"The crown," he said.

Xanthius handed him the crown. Archimedes put it in the water. The king did not seem to mind. He watched the water run over the top of the bowl.

Archimedes took the crown out. Xanthius dried it. With a pint measure Archimedes took more water out of the jug and poured it into the bowl. He counted the number of pints it took to fill the bowl to the top.

"The gold," Archimedes said.

The king gave it to him. Archimedes put the gold in the bowl. Again water ran over the sides. He took the gold out and poured in water from the pint measure. He did not have to add as much water as he had added for the crown.

"Well, Um?" Archimedes said to Xanthius.

Xanthius said at once, "Both the crown and the gold weigh the same. So if the crown was all gold, just as much water should have run out both times. More water ran out for the crown, so there is more metal in it than there should be. Some other metal was added to it."

"There is your answer," Archimedes told the king. "I will figure out how much silver was added."

The king said, "How is this boy doing? Do you want him to stay?"

"What boy?" Archimedes asked.

Xanthius was not going to show how bad he felt, not before the king. "This boy, sire," Xanthius said.

Archimedes laughed. "Ah, yes," he said.

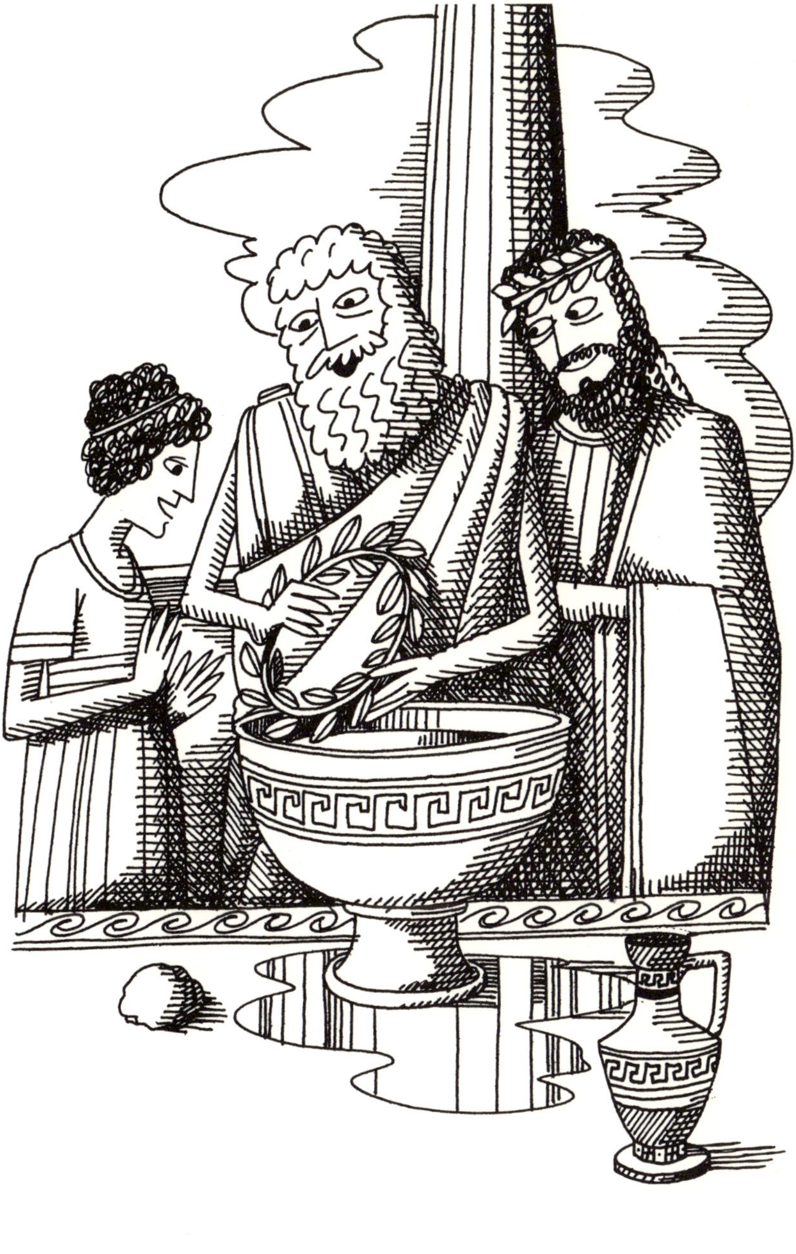

"Sometimes I forget he is a boy. He thinks before he opens his mouth. He is good to have around, and talking to him helps me think."

Xanthius was happy. To be of use to a man like Archimedes, even if Archimedes did not always know he was helping, was something. And he was learning so much from him.

"He is doing a job that men could not do," the king said, looking at Xanthius.

"Oh?" Archimedes said. "You must tell me about your work some time, Um."

As the king walked out, Archimedes walked with him.

"By the way," Xanthius heard Archimedes say, "how is that baby doing? The one I found. That boy said something or other about it a day or two ago."

"The baby is doing fine. Just fine," said the king.

EPILOGUE

Archimedes was a Greek mathematician who lived more than two thousand years ago. He was born in 287 B.C. in Syracuse, a city on an island called Sicily. Most of what we know about him comes from the writings of three men: Polybius, who was born about seven years after Archimedes died; Vitruvius, who lived in the first century B.C.; and Plutarch, who was born about two hundred and fifty years after Archimedes died. The information about Archimedes in this book, including the fact that he did not like to take baths, comes from these writings.

The slave Xanthius and his friend Droman are not found in the old writings. They have been added to the story. Slavery was part of the way of life in the Greek world, but unlike Xanthius, most slaves were captured in raids or wars on neighboring countries.

King Hiero II ruled until his death in 216 B.C. at the age of ninety. In 214 B.C. the Romans attacked Syracuse. Because of the war machines Archimedes had invented, it took the Romans two years to capture the city. Iron claws that came out from the walls of Syracuse picked up soldiers on land or ships at sea, raised them high, and let them drop. Archimedes himself directed the use of the machines.

Finally the Romans won the city. When their general, Marcellus, went back to Rome, he took with him the treasures of Syracuse. King Hiero's crown was probably among them.

Archimedes was killed when Syracuse was taken, in spite of Marcellus' orders to spare him. There are several stories about how he died. In one, a soldier came to take him to Marcellus. Archimedes was writing in the sand and would not go until he was done with the problem he was working on. The soldier grew angry and killed him. Another story has it that Archimedes was killed by soldiers who thought there was gold in a box he carried. He was seventy-five when he died.

Archimedes is still remembered as one of the greatest mathematicians in history. The answer to the crown problem led him to the Archimedean Principle: Anything put in water loses as much weight as the weight of the water it takes the place of.

ABOUT THE AUTHOR

Joan Lexau was delighted by the classic accounts of Archimedes' life, which portray him as a profound and gentle man, devoted to pure science and to the beauty of ideas. One ancient source tells us that Archimedes was often so lost in his thoughts that he forgot to eat, and occasionally he even had to be carried to the Baths. Miss Lexau felt that the account of his discovery in the Baths illustrated very well the fact that important ideas often come in homely and unexpected ways. All in all, she decided that a story about several events in the great mathematician's life was important to tell and would have special appeal to young readers.

Miss Lexau is the author of many distinguished books for children, and in 1962 she received the Children's Book Award from the Child Study Association for her novel *The Trouble with Terry*. Born in St. Paul, Minnesota, Miss Lexau now makes her home in New York City.

ABOUT THE ILLUSTRATOR

As a young boy, Salvatore Murdocca attended fine-arts classes on Saturdays at Pratt Institute in Brooklyn. He later studied at the High School of Art and Design and at the Art Students League. Mr. Murdocca received his first illustration commission at the age of nineteen. Two of his paintings received awards for excellence in a National Academy of Arts and Sciences Illustrators' Show.

Between free-lance assignments, Mr. Murdocca relaxes by painting in oils and by riding his ten-speed racing bike. He and his wife live in New York City.